FIRST EXPERIENCES

DIEGO'S VISIT TO THE DENTIST

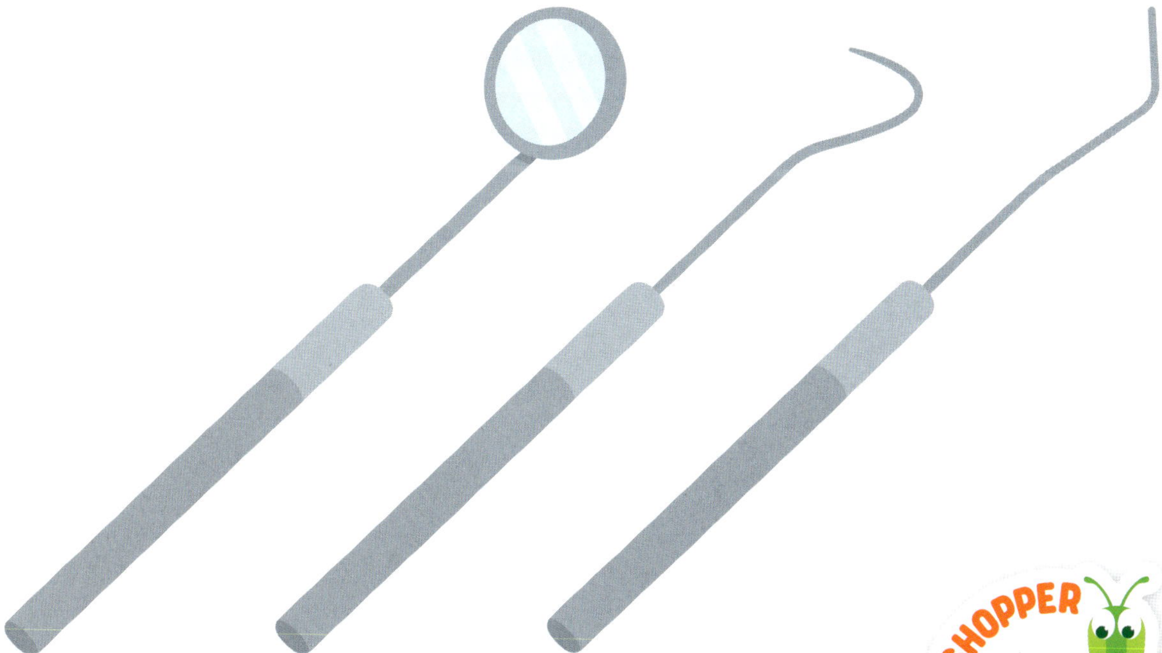

by Mari Schuh
illustrated by Daniela Massironi

Tools for Parents & Teachers

Grasshopper Books enhance imagination and introduce the earliest readers to fiction with fun storylines and illustrations. The easy-to-read text supports early reading experiences with repetitive sentence patterns and sight words.

Before Reading

- Look at the cover illustration. What do readers see? What do they think the book will be about?
- Look at the picture glossary together. Sound out the words. Ask readers to identify the first letter of each vocabulary word.

Read the Book

- "Walk" through the book, reading to or along with the reader. Point to the illustrations as you read.

After Reading

- Review the picture glossary again. Ask readers to locate the words in the text.
- Ask the reader: How did Diego feel before going to the dentist? How did he feel afterward? How do you know?

Grasshopper Books are published by Jump!
5357 Penn Avenue South
Minneapolis, MN 55419
www.jumplibrary.com

Library of Congress Cataloging-in-Publication Data

Names: Schuh, Mari C., 1975- author.
Massironi, Daniela, illustrator.
Title: Diego's visit to the dentist / by Mari Schuh;
illustrated by Daniela Massironi.
Description: Minneapolis, MN: Jump!, Inc., [2023]
Series: First experiences
Audience: Ages 4-7.
Identifiers: LCCN 2021059757 (print)
LCCN 2021059758 (ebook)
ISBN 9781636909240 (hardcover)
ISBN 9781636909257 (paperback)
ISBN 9781636909264 (ebook)
Subjects: LCSH: Readers (Primary)
Dentists–Juvenile fiction.
LCGFT: Readers (Publications)
Classification: LCC PE1119.2 .S373 2023 (print)
LCC PE1119.2 (ebook)
DDC 428.6/2–dc23/eng/20211215
LC record available at https://lccn.loc.gov/2021059757
LC ebook record available at https://lccn.loc.gov/2021059758

Editor: Jenna Gleisner
Direction and Layout: Anna Peterson
Illustrator: Daniela Massironi

Printed in the United States of America at
Corporate Graphics in North Mankato, Minnesota.

Table of Contents

Clean Teeth

"My teeth are good, Dad. I don't need to go to the dentist," I say.

“It’s OK to feel nervous, Diego,” Dad says.
“I will be with you. You can bring Ted, too.”

"My stomach feels funny," I say.

"Let's play while we wait," Dad says.

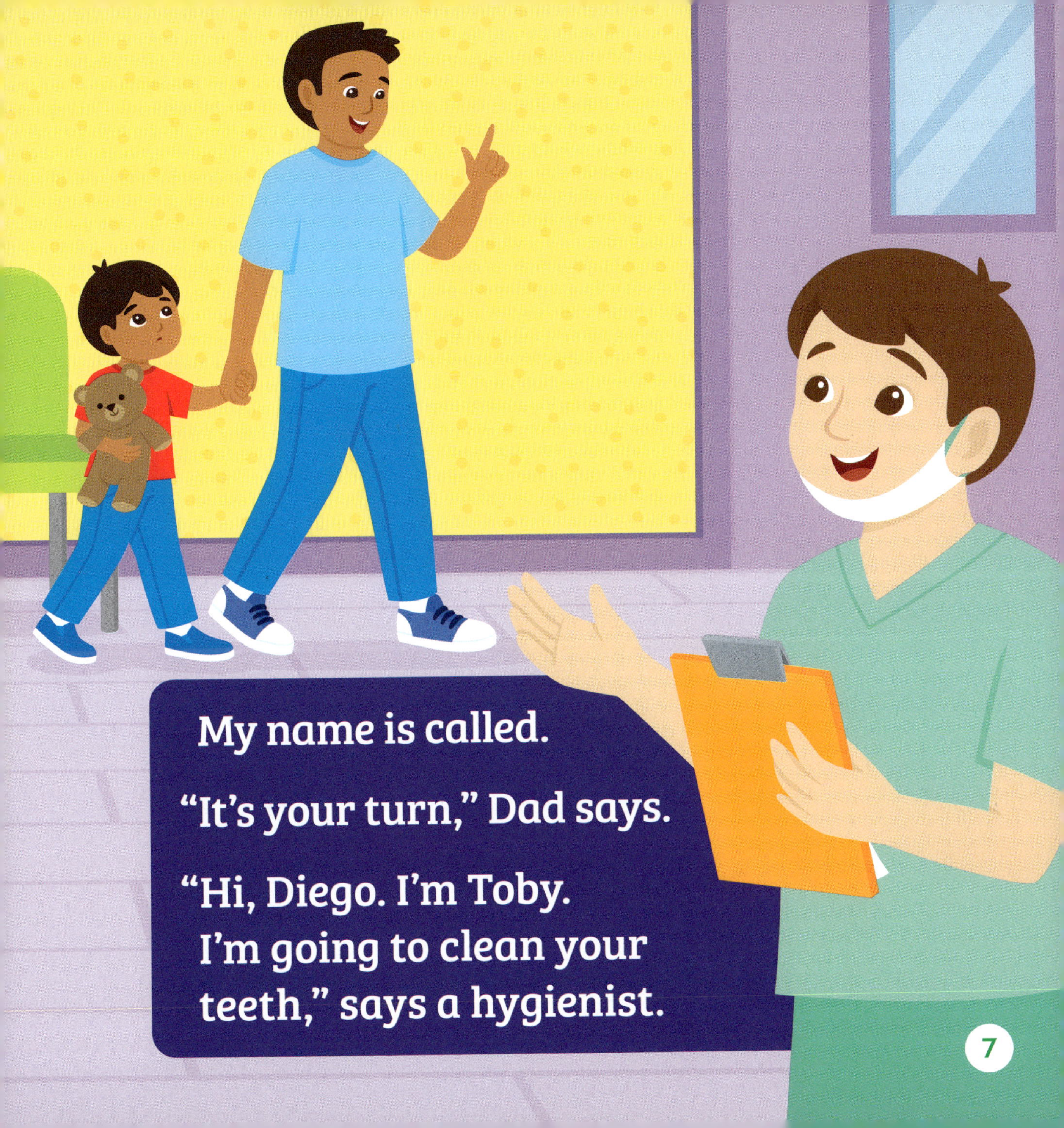

My name is called.

“It’s your turn,” Dad says.

“Hi, Diego. I’m Toby.
I’m going to clean your
teeth,” says a hygienist.

Toby turns a light on.

It is bright.

But it is not scary.

He just needs to see
my teeth.

"What are those?" I ask.

"My tools. They are small. They are made just for kids," Toby says.

tools

“This tool cleans teeth.
Ready, Diego?” Toby asks.

I nod.

Buzz!

It tickles!

Then the dentist comes in. She checks my teeth and gums.

"You take good care of your teeth, Diego. Keep it up!" she says.

Let's Review!

Diego was nervous to go to the dentist. What did he do to feel better before and during his visit?

A. ask questions B. sleep C. bring a toy D. read a book

Picture Glossary

dentist
A person who is trained to check, clean, and fix teeth.

gums
The firm, pink flesh around a person's teeth.

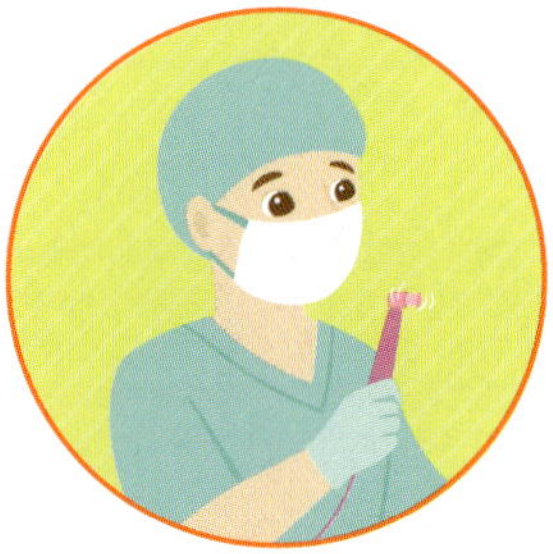

hygienist
A person who is trained to clean teeth, take X-rays, and help dentists.

nervous
Anxious or worried about something.

Let's Review! Answer Key: A. ask questions C. bring a toy